Math Expressions

Homework and Remembering • Volume 2

Developed by
The Children's Math Worlds Research Project

PROJECT DIRECTOR AND AUTHOR
Dr. Karen C. Fuson

This material is based upon work supported by the
National Science Foundation
under Grant Numbers
ESI-9816320, REC-9806020, and RED-935373.

Any opinions, findings, and conclusions, or recommendations expressed in this material
are those of the author and do not necessarily reflect the views of the National Science Foundation.

HOUGHTON MIFFLIN HARCOURT

Teacher Reviewers

Kindergarten
Patricia Stroh Sugiyama
Wilmette, Illinois

Barbara Wahle
Evanston, Illinois

Grade 1
Sandra Budson
Newton, Massachusetts

Janet Pecci
Chicago, Illinois

Megan Rees
Chicago, Illinois

Grade 2
Molly Dunn
Danvers, Massachusetts

Agnes Lesnick
Hillside, Illinois

Rita Soto
Chicago, Illinois

Grade 3
Jane Curran
Honesdale, Pennsylvania

Sandra Tucker
Chicago, Illinois

Grade 4
Sara Stoneberg Llibre
Chicago, Illinois

Sheri Roedel
Chicago, Illinois

Grade 5
Todd Atler
Chicago, Illinois

Leah Barry
Norfolk, Massachusetts

Special Thanks

Special thanks to the many teachers, students, parents, principals, writers, researchers, and work-study students who participated in the Children's Math Worlds Research Project over the years.

Credits

Cover art: (t) © Superstock/Alamy, (b) © Steve Bloom Images/Alamy
Illustrative art: Dave Klug
Technical art: Morgan-Cain & Associates

Printed in the U.S.A.

ISBN: 978-0-547-06690-5

10 11 12 1689 17 16 15 14

4500514306

Name _____ **Date** _____

Homework

Solve. Write the remainder as a whole number and as a fraction.

1. $4\overline{)9{,}813}$ 2. $3\overline{)3{,}712}$ 3. $5\overline{)7{,}082}$ 4. $2\overline{)6{,}129}$

5. $7\overline{)8{,}063}$ 6. $8\overline{)8{,}240}$ 7. $3\overline{)4{,}319}$ 8. $6\overline{)7{,}023}$

9. $5\overline{)8{,}115}$ 10. $9\overline{)10{,}909}$ 11. $7\overline{)9{,}315}$ 12. $9\overline{)10{,}542}$

Find the mean, median, and mode of each data set.

13. 31, 42, 34, 21, 33, 31

Mean: _____   Median: _____   Mode: _____

14. 561, 567, 561, 539

Mean: _____   Median: _____   Mode: _____

15. 4, 3, 2, 7, 6, 4, 7, 4, 8

Mean: _____   Median: _____   Mode: _____

Solve.

16. Hannah has four school workbooks. Their weights   *Show your work.*
    are 12 ounces, 14 ounces, 9 ounces, and 13 ounces.
    What is the mean weight of her workbooks?

    _____

17. Jose did 25 sit-ups on Monday, 20 on Tuesday,
    23 on Wednesday, 27 on Thursday, and 30 on Friday.
    What was the mean number of sit-ups he did?

    _____

18. Mrs. Kay works at a shoe store. Yesterday, she sold
    shoes in sizes 8, 6, 7, 9, 7, 8, and 5. What was the
    median shoe size she sold?

    _____

Remembering

This table shows the cards that 6 members of the Sports Card club have in their collections.

Club Member	Sport			
	Baseball	Basketball	Ice Hockey	Soccer
Alice	10	7	6	12
Kwami	0	35	15	0
Maureen	3	21	0	36
Nina	12	10	1	2
Ryan	30	8	18	24
Wally	20	28	12	15

1. Which member has 3 more ice hockey cards than Wally?

   _____

2. Write an additive comparison sentence to tell about the numbers of soccer cards that Alice and Wally have.

   _____

3. Which member has 10 times as many baseball cards as Maureen? _____

4. Write a multiplication comparison sentence to tell about the numbers of basketball cards that Alice and Wally have.

   _____

Write the metric unit you would use to measure each of the following.

5. Area of a field _____

6. Volume of a glass _____

7. Perimeter of a postcard _____

8. Distance between towns _____

Homework

Simplify each expression.

1. $11m - 9m =$ _____

2. $y + 8y =$ _____

3. $13s - s =$ _____

4. $d + 2d + d =$ _____

5. $(9b - b) - 2b =$ _____

6. $104z + z =$ _____

7. $21 - (10 - 5) =$ _____

8. $(900 - 100) - 100 =$ _____

9. $90 - (50 - 1) =$ _____

10. $18 \div (27 \div 9) =$ _____

11. $(63 \div 7) \div 9 =$ _____

12. $40 \div (36 \div 9) =$ _____

13. $(48 \div 6) \cdot (11 - 9) =$ _____

14. $(3 + 17) \div (16 - 12) =$ _____

15. $(15 + 10) - (50 \div 10) =$ _____

16. $(19 + 11) \div (9 - 6) =$ _____

Evaluate.

17. $c = 3$

   $4 \cdot (7 - c)$

   _____

18. $r = 2$

   $(42 \div 7) \cdot (r + 1)$

   _____

19. $w = 7$

   $(72 \div 9) \cdot w$

   _____

20. $m = 0$

   $(12 \div 3) \cdot (5 - m)$

   _____

21. $h = 14$

   $45 \div (h - 5)$

   _____

22. $p = 19$

   $(p + 1) \div (9 - 4)$

   _____

23. $v = 6$

   $(18 - 9) + (2 + v)$

   _____

24. $t = 1$

   $(7 \cdot 2) \div t$

   _____

25. $g = 10$

   $(g + 90) \div (17 - 13)$

   _____

Solve for $\square$ or n.

26. $7 \cdot (3 + 2) = 7 \cdot \square$

   $\square =$ _____

27. $(9 - 1) \cdot 4 = \square \cdot 4$

   $\square =$ _____

28. $8 \cdot (4 + 5) = \square \cdot 9$

   $\square =$ _____

29. $6 \cdot (8 - 8) = n$

   $n =$ _____

30. $(12 - 6) \div 3 = n$

   $n =$ _____

31. $(21 \div 7) \cdot (5 + 5) = n$

   $n =$ _____

Remembering

Divide.

1. $5\overline{)515}$ 2. $4\overline{)361}$ 3. $8\overline{)740}$ 4. $7\overline{)7,070}$

Write the place value of the underlined digit.

5. $5,\underline{6}16 =$ _____   6. $1\underline{3},044,652 =$ _____   7. $5\underline{9}1,756 =$ _____

Write an estimate to solve each problem.

8. What is a reasonable estimate of the product 9 × 99?

_____

9. What is a reasonable estimate of the quotient 4,181 ÷ 6?

_____

Solve.

10. Sarina has decided that the product of 59 and 100 is 59,000. Is Sarina's answer reasonable? Why or why not?

_____

_____

_____

11. Which rotation is a 90° counter-clockwise rotation of the letter V?

    $<$ $\wedge$ $\vee$ $>$

    A.   B.   C.   D.

        Properties and Algebraic Notation

Homework

Connections

Describe a situation involving division and a remainder in which you would round up.

_____

_____

_____

_____

_____

Representation

Use pictures to show the mean of the set of numbers 7, 5, and 3.

Communication

The Kite Club is divided into kite flying teams with 6 people on each team. There are 20 new people who want to join the club. Lupe says that not all of the teams will have an equal number of people. Is Lupe correct? Explain why or why not.

_____

_____

_____

_____

_____

Reasoning and Proof

Otis measures a field and finds its length to be 100 units. Jason measures the same field, using a different unit of measure. He finds the length to be 300 units. State the relationship between the two units of measure used. Explain.

_____

_____

_____

_____

_____

Name _____ **Date** _____

Remembering

Solve.

1. $9\overline{)37}$ 2. $6\overline{)40}$ 3. $5\overline{)23}$ 4. $7\overline{)50}$

5. $5\overline{)56}$ 6. $7\overline{)95}$ 7. $2\overline{)63}$ 8. $3\overline{)77}$

9. $4\overline{)86}$ 10. $6\overline{)75}$ 11. $8\overline{)94}$ 12. $4\overline{)97}$

13. $5\overline{)107}$ 14. $7\overline{)258}$ 15. $4\overline{)389}$ 16. $2\overline{)135}$

17. $5\overline{)641}$ 18. $3\overline{)947}$ 19. $6\overline{)816}$ 20. $8\overline{)905}$

21. $6\overline{)3,716}$ 22. $4\overline{)3,843}$ 23. $7\overline{)5,479}$ 24. $3\overline{)1,964}$

Write the metric unit you would use to measure each of the following.

25. perimeter of a field

_____

26. area of a state

_____

27. mass of a dog

_____

28. length of a pencil

_____

Use Mathematical Processes

Name   **Date**

Homework

The patterns below involve one operation. Describe each pattern, and identify the next term in it.

1. 2, 6, 18, 54, 162, 486, ... _____

2. 975, 925, 875, 825, 775, 725, ... _____

3. 4,000, 2,000, 1,000, 500, 250, ... _____

4. 115, 145, 175, 205, 235, 265, ... _____

5. 246, 211, 176, 141, 106, 71, ... _____

The patterns below involve two operations. Describe each pattern, and identify the next two terms in it.

6. 1, 2, 4, 8, 10, 20, 22, ... _____

7. 5, 10, 6, 11, 7, 12, 8, ... _____

8. 3, 4, 8, 9, 18, 19, 38, ... _____

9. 4, 2, 6, 4, 12, 10, 30, ... _____

Solve.

10. A store owner gave each customer a number. He created a pattern to choose numbers, and gave a prize to the customers with these numbers. So far, he called numbers 1, 3, 9, 27, and 81. What are the next two numbers that will be called? Explain how you found your answer.

_____

_____

_____

Remembering

Multiply.

1. 48 × 6 = _____   **2.** 496 × 5 = _____   **3.** 54 × 11 = _____

Divide.

4. 88 ÷ 9 = _____   **5.** 917 ÷ 7 = _____   **6.** 4,187 ÷ 8 = _____

Find a reasonable estimate for each problem.

7. 38 × 24 _____   **8.** 524 ÷ 6 _____

Evaluate.

9. $a = 8$ **10.** $c = 5$ **11.** $w = 10$

$(7 + a) - 3$ _____ $(8 ÷ 4) \cdot (c - 2)$ _____ $(36 ÷ 4) \cdot w$ _____

Solve.

12. Ken buys 3 packages of tomato seeds. Each package has 16 seeds. He plants an equal amount of seeds in 4 rows of his garden. How many tomato seeds does Ken plant in each row of his garden? _____

13. Which two figures look congruent? Explain how you know.

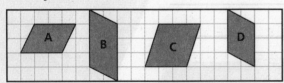

_____

_____

Numerical Patterns

Homework

Use the operation or operations to complete the table.

1.

Add 9					
Input		2			1.
Output	12		18	14	

2.

Subtract 6, then multiply by 2					
Input	10	8	11	7	9
Output					

Use the table to complete exercises 3 and 4.

Number of Boxes (b)	1	2	3	4	5	6	7	8
Number of Crayons (c)	6	12	18	24	30	36	42	48

3. Using words, write the rule of the function.

_____

4. Using the variables b and c, write an equation
which shows that the number of crayons (c) is a function
of the number of boxes (b).

_____

Solve.

5. Below the table, write an equation that uses
the variables x and y and shows y as a function of x.

x	4	5	6	7	8
y	1	2	3	4	5

_____

6. Each student brought in 9 cans to recycle. Write
an equation to represent the total number of cans
(c) for any number of students (s).

_____

Name _____ **Date** _____

Remembering

Multiply.

1. 71
× 5

2. 403
×   7

3. 58
× 31

Divide.

4. 6)92

5. 3)422

6. 9)9,828

Find the mean, median, mode, and range of each data set.

7. 3, 6, 2, 3, 8, 2

Mean: _____   Median: _____

Mode: _____   Range: _____

8. 10, 15, 10, 13, 11, 15, 10

Mean: _____   Median: _____

Mode: _____   Range: _____

Solve for the variable in each equation.

9. $n + 5 = 36$

$n =$ _____

10. $m \div 8 = 30$

$m =$ _____

11. $6w = 30$

$w =$ _____

Decide if the pair of figures appears to be similar.
Write _yes_ or _no_. Explain how you know.

12.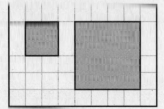

_____

_____

13.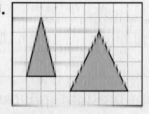

_____

_____

Use the coordinate plane below to answer the questions that follow.

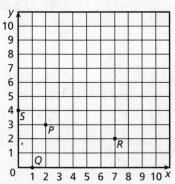

Write an ordered pair to represent the location of each point.

1. point P _____   **2.** point Q _____   **3.** point R _____   **4.** point S _____

Plot and label a point at each location.

5. point W at (3, 9)   **6.** point X at (3, 5)   **7.** point Y at (9, 5)

Solve.

8. Suppose points W, X, and Y, represent three vertices
of rectangle WXYZ. Where should point Z be plotted
to form the rectangle?

_____

Plot and label point Z. Then use a ruler to draw
the rectangle.

9. What ordered pair represents the point at the center
of the rectangle?

_____

10. Explain how subtraction can be used to find the lengths
of line segment WX and line segment XY.

_____

_____

_____

Name _____ Date _____

Remembering

Divide.

1. $4\overline{)820}$ 2. $8\overline{)250}$ 3. $2\overline{)125}$ 4. $5\overline{)5,615}$

Simplify each expression.

5. $(54 \div 9) \cdot (12 - 4) =$ _____

6. $(8 + 7) \div (15 - 10) =$ _____

7. $(6 + 5) - (70 \div 7) =$ _____

8. $(23 - 17) + (3 \cdot 2) =$ _____

9. Write the prime factorization of 45. _____

10. Explain why 45 is a multiple of each factor you wrote for exercise 9.

_____

11. Is 29 a prime number? Explain why or why not.

_____

Write an estimate to solve each problem.

12. What is a reasonable estimate of the sum $18,759 + 31,044$?

_____

13. What is a reasonable estimate of the difference $6,052 - 978$?

_____

Solve.

14. DeJuan has decided that the product of 43 and 1,000 is 4,300. Is DeJuan's answer reasonable? Why or why not?

_____

_____

Homework

1. Complete the function table.

2. Write the rule of the function table, using words.

_____

3. Using the variables *x* and *y*, write an equation that shows that *y* is a function of *x*.

_____

x	y
0	0
1	2
2	4
3	
	8
5	

4. Each ordered pair in the table represents a point. Use the table to write each set of ordered pairs.

_____

5. On the coordinate plane at the right, use the ordered pairs to plot and label each point. Then use a ruler and draw a segment to connect the points.

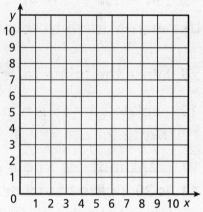

6. Compare the *y*-coordinate of each point to its *x*-coordinate. Describe the relationship, using words.

_____

7. How does the pattern on the coordinate plane compare to the pattern in the function table?

_____

8. What is the *y*-coordinate of a point on the line graph if the *x*-coordinate is 8? Explain how you found your answer.

_____

Name _____   **Date** _____

Remembering

Multiply.

1. $36 \times 5 =$ _____

2. $245 \times 3 =$ _____

3. $24 \times 23 =$ _____

Divide.

4. $4\overline{)97}$

5. $3\overline{)749}$

6. $7\overline{)8,467}$

Use mental math to solve for the variable in each equation.

7. $3n - 5 = 7$

  $n =$ _____

8. $4m + 8 = 16$

  $m =$ _____

9. $(a \div 3) - 4 = 6$

  $a =$ _____

Solve.

10. Franklin takes 1 hour 45 minutes to get to work. He has to be at work at 6:30 P.M. What time should Franklin leave to get to work? _____

11. There are 85 students sitting in the bleachers. Each row of the bleachers seats 7 students. How many rows of the bleachers will the students be sitting in? _____

12. Estimate the area of the pond in square units. Explain how you found your estimate.

_____

_____

_____

_____

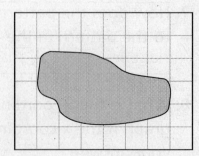

Graph a Function

Name _____ Date _____

Homework

This table shows continuous data. Use the table for exercises 1–3.

1. Is the trend of data increasing or decreasing? Explain your answer.

   _____

   _____

   _____

Morning Temperatures	
Time	**Temperature (°F)**
12 A.M.	44
2 A.M.	43
4 A.M.	40
6 A.M.	38
8 A.M.	38

2. Could you use the given data to predict the temperature at 5 A.M.? Explain your answer.

   _____

   _____

3. If you create a line graph from the data, what will the line look like between 4 A.M. and 6 A.M.?

   _____

Use the graph for exercises 4 and 5.

4. List the distance traveled at each hour.

   _____

   _____

5. Explain what could have happened between hours 4 and 5. Support your answer.

   _____

   _____

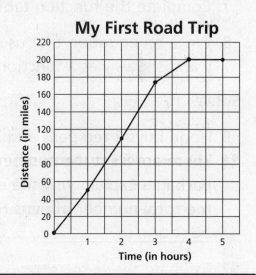

My First Road Trip

6. On a separate sheet of grid paper, make a line graph that displays the data in the table.

My Second Road Trip	
Time (hours)	**Distance (miles)**
0	0
1	60
2	130
3	190
4	200

Name _____ **Date** _____

Remembering

Multiply.

1. 64 × 9 = _____
2. 387 × 6 = _____
3. 74 × 58 = _____

Divide.

4. 54 ÷ 7 = _____
5. 389 ÷ 4 = _____
6. 3,284 ÷ 4 = _____

Use the function table for exercises 7 and 8.

x	3	4	5	6	7	8	
y	12	16	20	24	28		40

7. Complete the function table.

8. Write an equation that uses the variables x and y and shows y as a function of x. _____

Solve.

9. Hoon buys 2 red pens and 3 packages of blue pens. Let a represent the number of blue pens in each package. Explain why the equation $3a + 2$ represents the total number of pens Hoon bought.

   _____

   _____

10. Look at Figure A. Circle the shaded figure below that shows how Figure A looks after it is rotated 270° clockwise.

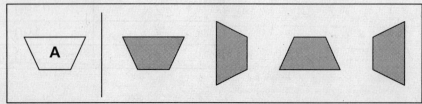

Read a Line Graph

Name _____ **Date** _____

Homework

Add.

1. $3\frac{2}{6}$
$+\ 6\frac{3}{6}$

2. $8\frac{5}{10}$
$+\ 9\frac{6}{10}$

3. $7\frac{3}{4}$
$+\ 4\frac{2}{4}$

4. $1\frac{5}{9}$
$+\ 5\frac{7}{9}$

Subtract.

5. $7\frac{2}{3}$
$-\ 3\frac{1}{3}$

6. $8\frac{2}{7}$
$-\ 5\frac{5}{7}$

7. $6\frac{1}{4}$
$-\ 2\frac{3}{4}$

8. $9\frac{1}{8}$
$-\ 4\frac{5}{8}$

Add or subtract.

9. $\frac{1}{4} + \frac{7}{4} =$ _____

10. $\frac{3}{8} + \frac{6}{8} =$ _____

11. $\frac{9}{6} - \frac{8}{6} =$ _____

12. $\frac{5}{9} + \frac{6}{9} =$ _____

13. $\frac{9}{2} - \frac{6}{2} =$ _____

14. $\frac{5}{10} - \frac{2}{10} =$ _____

15. $\frac{2}{5} + \frac{4}{5} =$ _____

16. $\frac{8}{7} - \frac{3}{7} =$ _____

17. $\frac{7}{3} - \frac{2}{3} =$ _____

18. Write and solve a mixed number word problem.

_____

_____

_____

_____

_____

_____

_____

_____

_____

_____

Remembering

Solve.

1. 653 + 15,710 = _____   **2.** 85,132 − 6,409 = _____   **3.** 67 × 45 = _____

4. 784 ÷ 4 = _____   **5.** 8,147 + 54,479 = _____   **6.** 81,656 − 1,639 = _____

7. 39 × 76 = _____   **8.** 8,931 ÷ 6 = _____   **9.** 32,910 + 2,319 = _____

10. 65,325 − 8,607 = _____   **11.** 82 × 61 = _____   **12.** 9,424 ÷ 9 = _____

Solve.

Show your work.

13. The school baseball team played 56 games. They scored a mean (average) of 4 runs in each game. How many runs did they score in all?

_____

14. Matt collects football cards. His album holds 9 cards on each page. If he has 125 cards for his album, what is the greatest number of pages he can fill?

_____

Find the area and perimeter of each triangle.

15.

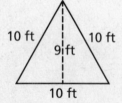

Area: _____

Perimeter: _____

16.

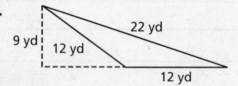

Area: _____

Perimeter: _____

Solve for the variable in each equation.

17. $r \div 5 = 35$

$r =$ _____

18. $p - 4 = 23$

$p =$ _____

19. $9w = 36$

$w =$ _____

Add and Subtract Mixed Numbers With Like Denominators

Name _____ Date _____

Homework

Insert > or < to make a true statement.

1. $\frac{2}{3}$ ◯ $\frac{2}{4}$ 2. $\frac{5}{8}$ ◯ $\frac{5}{7}$ 3. $\frac{3}{5}$ ◯ $\frac{3}{6}$

4. $\frac{7}{9}$ ◯ $\frac{8}{9}$ 5. $\frac{5}{11}$ ◯ $\frac{6}{11}$ 6. $\frac{4}{7}$ ◯ $\frac{3}{7}$

Write each mixed number as an improper fraction.

7. $6\frac{5}{8} =$ 8. $2\frac{1}{4} =$

9. $8\frac{3}{10} =$ 10. $4\frac{2}{6} =$

Write each improper fraction as a mixed number.

11. $\frac{26}{3} =$ 12. $\frac{47}{7} =$

13. $\frac{59}{9} =$ 14. $\frac{44}{5} =$

Add or subtract.

15. $\frac{2}{3} + \frac{2}{3} =$ 16. $\frac{4}{10} + \frac{12}{10} =$ 17. $\frac{5}{7} - \frac{3}{7} =$

18. $1\frac{3}{9} + \frac{7}{9} =$ 19. $\frac{3}{4} + 3\frac{3}{4} =$ 20. $2\frac{4}{15} - \frac{10}{15} =$

21. $\frac{6}{12} + \frac{5}{12} =$ 22. $\frac{15}{20} - \frac{6}{20} =$ 23. $3\frac{3}{5} - 3\frac{1}{5} =$

24. $\frac{3}{6} + 2\frac{6}{6} =$ 25. $2\frac{7}{8} - 1\frac{2}{8} =$ 26. $1\frac{8}{11} - \frac{10}{11} =$

Remembering

Solve these problems about Mellie's Deli sandwiches.

Mellie's Deli

Regular (serves 2) _____ $3.00
Friendship (serves 4) _____ $5.00
Super (serves 10) _____ $12.00
Magna (serves 18) _____ $20.00

1. Suppose 5 friends each want 1 serving of a sandwich. How many Regular sandwiches will they need? If they ordered Friendship sandwiches, how many would they need?

_____

_____

2. Ten friends go to Mellie's after a soccer game and order 3 Friendship sandwiches. If each person has 1 sandwich serving, what fraction of the Friendship sandwiches will they eat all together?

_____

3. There will be 25 people at Morey's graduation party. Should Morey order Super or Magna sandwiches? Explain your thinking.

_____

_____

_____

4. Draw and label a right angle, an acute angle, and an obtuse angle.

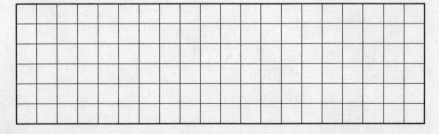

Practice With Fractions

Name _____ **Date** _____

Homework

Insert <, >, or = to make a true statement

1. $\frac{5}{6} \bigcirc \frac{9}{10}$

2. $\frac{2}{5} \bigcirc \frac{4}{16}$

3. $\frac{7}{5} \bigcirc \frac{5}{3}$

4. $\frac{6}{7} \bigcirc \frac{4}{6}$

5. $\frac{7}{8} \bigcirc \frac{10}{12}$

6. $\frac{3}{4} \bigcirc \frac{8}{12}$

Add or subtract.

7. $\frac{3}{6} + \frac{4}{8} =$

8. $\frac{2}{4} + \frac{9}{10} =$

9. $\frac{4}{5} - \frac{5}{7} =$

10. $\frac{2}{5} + \frac{2}{9} =$

11. $\frac{6}{7} + \frac{1}{3} =$

12. $\frac{4}{9} - \frac{1}{5} =$

13. $\frac{1}{4} + \frac{2}{7} =$

14. $\frac{7}{9} - \frac{2}{6} =$

15. $\frac{7}{8} - \frac{3}{4} =$

16. $\frac{1}{2} + \frac{7}{10} =$

17. $\frac{5}{8} - \frac{3}{5} =$

18. $\frac{5}{6} - \frac{4}{10} =$

Find the simplest equivalent fraction.

19. $\frac{20}{30} =$ _____

20. $\frac{18}{42} =$ _____

21. $\frac{10}{18} =$ _____

22. $\frac{18}{24} =$ _____

23. $\frac{18}{36} =$ _____

24. $\frac{42}{48} =$ _____

25. $\frac{10}{24} =$ _____

26. $\frac{36}{48} =$ _____

27. $\frac{21}{28} =$ _____

Remembering

Write each mixed number as an improper fraction.

1. $2\frac{2}{15} = \frac{}{15}$ 　　　　　**2.** $1\frac{3}{4} = \frac{}{4}$ 　　　　　**3.** $6\frac{7}{10} = \frac{}{10}$

4. $5\frac{1}{2} = \frac{}{2}$ 　　　　　**5.** $3\frac{5}{8} = \frac{}{8}$ 　　　　　**6.** $4\frac{5}{6} = \frac{}{6}$

Write each improper fraction as a mixed number.

7. $\frac{21}{12} = $ _____ 　　　**8.** $\frac{14}{3} = $ _____ 　　　**9.** $\frac{31}{9} = $ _____

10. $\frac{45}{7} = $ _____ 　　**11.** $\frac{44}{20} = $ _____ 　　**12.** $\frac{28}{5} = $ _____

The Fin and Fur Pet Shop has 35 puppies ready for adoption. Solve each problem about the puppies.

Show your work.

13. Twenty of the puppies are housebroken. What fraction are housebroken?

_____

14. If $\frac{3}{5}$ of the puppies are terriers, what fraction are not terriers?

_____

15. Maggie walked $\frac{2}{7}$ of the puppies. Josh walked $\frac{1}{5}$ of the puppies. What fraction of the puppies did they walk altogether?

_____

16. Jing fed $\frac{3}{7}$ of the puppies. Theo fed $\frac{2}{5}$ of the puppies. Who fed fewer puppies? How many fewer?

_____

Complete each row.

	Millimeters	Centimeters	Decimeters	Meters
17.	40	4	_____	0.04
18.	_____	30	3	0.3
19.	7,500	750	75	_____

　　　　　　　　　　　Practice With Unlike Denominators

Homework

Name each figure. Describe what makes each figure different from the others.

1.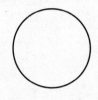

2.

3.

4.

_____   _____   _____   _____

_____   _____   _____   _____

_____   _____   _____   _____

_____   _____   _____   _____

Write the number of cubes in each stack.

5.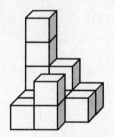

6.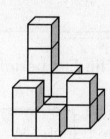

7.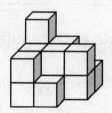

_____   _____   _____

Can you fold each net to make a cube? Write *yes* or *no*. If necessary, test the nets by tracing them on paper and cutting them out and making a cube.

8.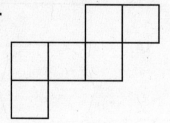

9.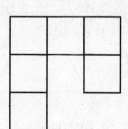

10.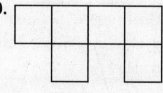

_____   _____   _____

Remembering

Solve. *Show your work.*

1. $1\frac{2}{3} + 2\frac{1}{3} =$ _____

2. $3\frac{4}{5} - 2\frac{1}{5} =$ _____

3. $2\frac{3}{8} + 2\frac{7}{8} =$ _____

4. $4\frac{1}{6} + 1\frac{5}{6} =$ _____

5. $1\frac{3}{10} + 2\frac{7}{10} =$ _____

6. $5\frac{1}{4} - 4\frac{3}{4} =$ _____

7. A DVD machine can duplicate one disc every 3 seconds. At this rate, how many discs can the machine duplicate in 1 hour?

_____

8. A CD holds 80 minutes of music. If each song on the CD is an average of 3 minutes, about how many songs can fit on the CD?

_____

Name each regular polygon and find its perimeter.

9.
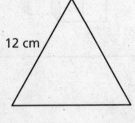
12 cm

_____

_____

10.
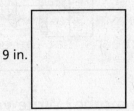
9 in.

_____

_____

11.
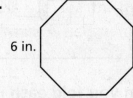
6 in.

_____

_____

12.
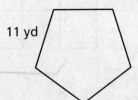
11 yd

_____

_____

13.
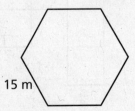
15 m

_____

_____

14.
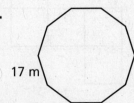
17 m

_____

_____

Spheres and Cubes

Name _____ **Date** _____

Remembering

Complete each number sentence. Show your work on a separate sheet of paper.

1. 1,326 + 456,106 = _____

2. 8,215,005 − 23,749 = _____

3. 7 × 634 = _____

4. 87 ÷ 7 = _____

5. 63,808 + 4,775,096 = _____

6. 912,634 − 8,856 = _____

7. 91 × 28 = _____

8. 917 ÷ 5 = _____

9. 536,697 + 14,194 = _____

10. 503,652 − 46,847 = _____

11. 18 × 39 = _____

12. 639 ÷ 9 = _____

Find the perimeter of each regular polygon.

13.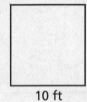

14.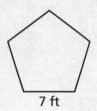

15.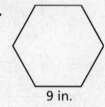

16.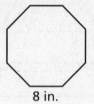

10 ft   7 ft   9 in.   8 in.

_____   _____   _____   _____

Find the perimeter and area of each figure. Show your work.

17.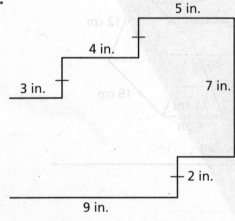

18.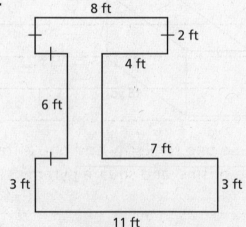

P = _____

A = _____

P = _____

A = _____

Name each solid. Also name the base, where possible.

1.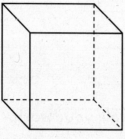

_____

_____

2.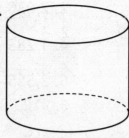

_____

_____

3.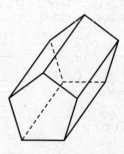

_____

_____

4.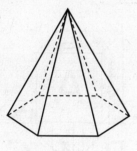

_____

_____

5.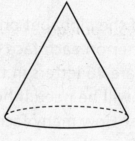

_____

_____

6.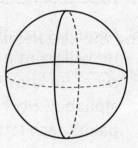

_____

_____

7. Describe one similarity and one difference among spheres, cones, and cylinders.

_____

_____

_____

_____

8. Describe one similarity and one difference among cubes, square prisms, and square pyramids.

_____

_____

_____

_____

_____

Name _____ **Date** _____

Remembering

Divide. Show your work on a separate sheet of paper.

1. 5,232 ÷ 6 = _____

2. 2,036 ÷ 4 = _____

3. 4,945 ÷ 5 = _____

4. 1,285 ÷ 3 = _____

5. 5,855 ÷ 9 = _____

6. 3,555 ÷ 7 = _____

Solve.   *Show your work.*

7. The surface area of a cube is 1,950 sq cm. What is
the area of each face of the cube?

_____

8. Miguel is painting letters of the alphabet on cubes.
He will paint a different letter on each face of each
cube. He knows that there are 26 letters in the
alphabet. How many cubes will he need if he
paints each letter only once? How many faces on
the last cube will be empty?

_____

Describe each figure using geometry language.

9.

10.

11.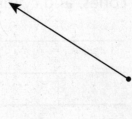

_____

_____

_____

12.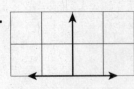

13.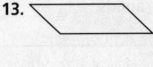

14.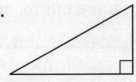

_____

_____

_____

Compare and Contrast Solids

Name _____ **Date** _____

Remembering

Multiply.

1. $79 \times 4 =$ _____

2. $871 \times 5 =$ _____

3. $92 \times 78 =$ _____

Divide.

4. $90 \div 6 =$ _____

5. $486 \div 5 =$ _____

6. $4{,}036 \div 3 =$ _____

Simplify each expression.

7. $24 - 6 \cdot 2 =$ _____

8. $7 + 3 \cdot (2 + 5) =$ _____

9. $(9c + 4c) - 7c =$ _____

Solve.

10. Ms. Scott bought 3 packages with 24 pens
in each package. After she gave each of
her students three pens, she had 12 pens left.
How many students does Ms. Scott have?

_____

11. Monica left school at 4:45 P.M. She had basketball
practice for 1 hour and 15 minutes and classes for
7 hours. At what time did school start?

_____

Use a protractor to measure each angle.

12.

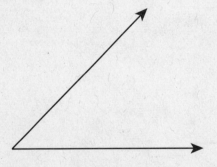

_____

13.

_____

Estimate Using Benchmarks

Homework

1. Connections

At a track meet, four people jumped in a high jump event. Jason jumped 1.02 meters. Eric jumped 0.98 meters. Pedro jumped 1.24 meters. Ken jumped 1.2 meters. Order the contestants from highest jump to lowest.

_____

2. Reasoning and Proof

Mori is thinking of a number with two decimal places that is less than 1. The digit in the tenths place is an odd number. The digit in the hundredths place is 7 less than the digit in the tenths place. What number is Mori thinking of? Explain your reasoning.

_____

3. Communication

Bill says that only some zeros in decimal number are important. Is Bill correct? Explain why or why not.

_____

_____

4. Representation

Susan rounded 0.9 to 0.10 on a math test. Did she round correctly? Use pictures to help explain your answer.

_____

Name _____ **Date** _____

Remembering

Divide. Write the quotient with a remainder.

1. 5)3,843

2. 4)4,502

3. 3)1,795

4. 7)7,377

5. 6)1,788

6. 5)3,823

Solve.

7. Jason has 252 boxes. He wants to place 6 books in each box. How many boxes will he fill?

_____

8. Lupe has 220 photos from her vacation. She wants to place them in a photo album and can put 9 photos on a page. How many pages will she fill?

_____

Find the perimeter and area of each figure.

9.

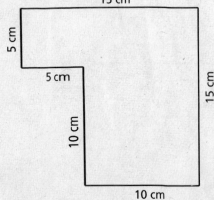

Perimeter: _____

Area: _____

10.

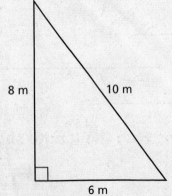

Perimeter: _____

Area: _____

Use Mathematical Processes

Name _____ **Date** _____

Homework

Write the measurement marked on each ruler.

1.

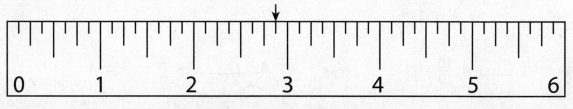

2.

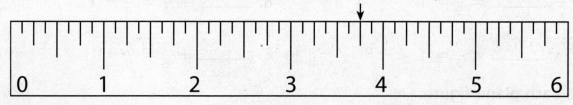

3.

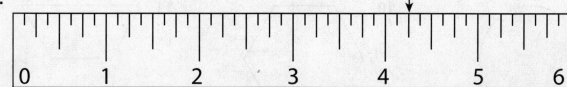

Measure each line segment to the nearest $\frac{1}{8}$ inch.

4. •————————————•

_____

5. •—————————————————————————————•

_____

6. •————————————————————•

_____

7. •————————————————————————————————•

_____

Draw a line segment with the length shown.

8. $4\frac{7}{8}$ inches

9. $2\frac{3}{8}$ inches

10. $3\frac{1}{2}$ inches

Remembering

Complete each equation.

1. $\frac{2}{5} + $ _____ $= \frac{5}{5} = 1$

2. _____ $+ \frac{7}{12} = \frac{12}{12} = 1$

3. $\frac{8}{10} + $ _____ $= \frac{10}{10} = 1$

4. _____ $+ \frac{4}{6} = \frac{6}{6} = 1$

5. $\frac{5}{9} + $ _____ $= \frac{9}{9} = 1$

6. _____ $+ \frac{3}{4} = \frac{4}{4} = 1$

7. $\frac{6}{7} + $ _____ $= \frac{7}{7} = 1$

8. _____ $+ \frac{1}{8} = \frac{8}{8} = 1$

Name each plane figure.

9.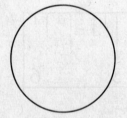

_____

10.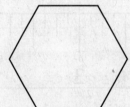

_____

11.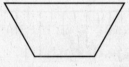

_____

Name each solid.

12.

_____

13.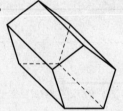

_____

14.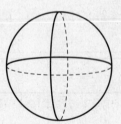

_____

Solve.

15. Amanda checked out 7 books with 64 pages each. She also checked out 4 books with 89 pages each. How many total pages is Amanda going to read?

_____

Length

Homework

Solve.

Show your work.

1. Denzel's father installed carpet tiles in the family room. The room is 12 feet by 16 feet. Each tile measured 1 square foot. How many tiles did he use?

_____

2. Brady built a doghouse for his new puppy. The inside of the doghouse measured 2 feet wide, 3 feet deep, and 4 feet tall. How many cubic feet of space are inside the doghouse?

_____

3. A play area measures 20 yards long and 15 yards wide. It costs $2.00 per square yard to cover the area with wood chips. What is the cost of new wood chips for the entire play area?

_____

4. Awan keeps his art supplies in a special box. The box is 18 inches long, 9 inches wide, and 6 inches deep. How many cubic inches of space are inside the box?

_____

Solve each problem about objects in your home.

5. Measure the area of an object at home. Name the object and the unit or units you used to measure its area.

_____

_____

6. Measure the volume of an object at home. Name the object and the unit or units you used to measure its volume.

_____

_____

Name _____ **Date** _____

Remembering

Write a > or < to compare the fractions.

1. $\frac{3}{6}$ ___ $\frac{3}{5}$

2. $\frac{6}{10}$ ___ $\frac{7}{10}$

3. $\frac{2}{3}$ ___ $\frac{2}{4}$

4. $\frac{4}{7}$ ___ $\frac{3}{7}$

5. $\frac{3}{9}$ ___ $\frac{3}{8}$

6. $\frac{10}{15}$ ___ $\frac{9}{15}$

Add or subtract.

7. $\frac{2}{9} + \frac{5}{9} =$ _____

8. $\frac{2}{5} + 3\frac{1}{5} =$ _____

9. $1\frac{4}{10} - \frac{9}{10} =$ _____

10. $2\frac{3}{4} + \frac{3}{8} =$ _____

11. $\frac{3}{2} + \frac{2}{5} =$ _____

12. $5\frac{1}{6} - 1\frac{2}{3} =$ _____

How many cubes can you see in each stack?
How many cubes can you not see?
How many cubes total are in each stack?

13.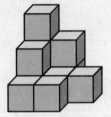

14.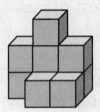

15.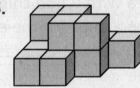

___ cubes can be
seen

___ cubes can be
seen

___ cubes can be
seen

___ cubes cannot be
seen

___ cube cannot be
seen

___ cubes cannot be
seen

___ cubes total

___ cubes total

___ cubes total

16. Inez bought 3 pairs of socks for $2.35 each and a hat for
$6.95. She paid with a $20 bill. How much change should
she receive?

_____

17. Ali received $5.65 change from a $20 bill. He bought a
present for $11.95 and a card. What was the cost of
the card?

_____

Square and Cubic Measurement

Homework

Solve. Remember: 1 pound = 16 ounces.

Show your work.

1. A female rabbit gave birth to 6 babies. Each baby weighed 4 ounces. How many ounces did the babies weigh in all?

_____

2. One watermelon weighs 8 pounds 2 ounces. Another weighs 7 pounds 12 ounces. Which watermelon is heavier? By how many ounces?

_____

3. A box of cereal weighs 21 ounces. Does it weigh more or less than 1 pound? How much more or less?

_____

4. At the beginning of the school year, Jared's dog weighed $46\frac{1}{2}$ pounds. At the end of the school year, it weighed 50 pounds. How much weight did Jared's dog gain during that time? How many ounces is this?

_____

5. Claire has 8 books. Each book weighs 8 ounces. How many pounds do her books weigh altogether?

_____

6. A bread recipe calls for $6\frac{1}{4}$ pounds of flour. How many batches of bread can a baker make with 25 pounds of flour?

_____

Remembering

Solve on a separate sheet of paper.

1. $5\overline{)93}$ 2. $9\overline{)513}$ 3. $7\overline{)764}$ 4. $8\overline{)7,235}$

5. $4\overline{)54}$ 6. $6\overline{)624}$ 7. $4\overline{)861}$ 8. $6\overline{)9,387}$

9. $7\overline{)75}$ 10. $2\overline{)734}$ 11. $3\overline{)970}$ 12. $2\overline{)5,678}$

13. $3\overline{)66}$ 14. $8\overline{)538}$ 15. $5\overline{)477}$ 16. $9\overline{)7,805}$

17. Check two of your divisions by multiplying and adding the remainder.

_____

Is each figure a net for a cube? Write yes or no.

18.   19. 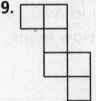   20.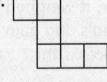

_____   _____   _____

Solve.   *Show your work.*

21. There are 6 pennies, 5 dimes, and 4 quarters in Josela's pocket. What fraction of the coins are pennies?

_____

22. Luis and Sasha have identical notebooks. Luis's notebook is $\frac{3}{4}$ full. Sasha's notebook is $\frac{5}{8}$ full. Whose notebook has less space remaining?

_____

Name _____ **Date** _____

Homework

Percy and Grace are making a birthday cake for their father. Their only measuring container holds $\frac{1}{4}$ cup.

Solve.

Show your work.

1. They need 2 cups of flour. How many $\frac{1}{4}$ cups should they measure?

   _____

2. They need $1\frac{1}{2}$ cups of sugar. How many $\frac{1}{4}$ cups should they measure?

   _____

3. The recipe calls for $\frac{3}{4}$ cup of cocoa. How many $\frac{1}{4}$ cups of cocoa should they measure?

   _____

4. The recipe calls for $\frac{1}{8}$ cup of oil. How can they use their $\frac{1}{4}$ cup to measure the oil they need?

   _____

5. Write and solve your own measurement word problem that uses fractions.

   _____

   _____

   _____

   _____

   _____

   _____

Remembering

Solve on a separate sheet of paper.

1. 37,619 + 24,850

2. 867,027 − 9,436

3. 630,631 − 9,747

4. 2,604,925 + 3,687

5. 437,025 − 18,094

6. 320,705 − 56,923

7. 17,491 + 820,623

8. 7,586,742 − 87,604

9. 746,502 − 75,575

Name each triangle by letters, angles, and sides.

10.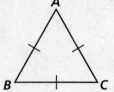

_____

_____

_____

11.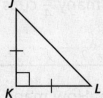

_____

_____

_____

12.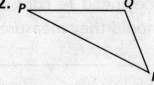

_____

_____

_____

Make a sketch to match the description.

13. intersecting lines

14. parallel lines

15. perpendicular lines

Solve.

16. In how many different ways can Dwayne, Peter, and Marta stand in a line?

_____

17. Five teams are competing in a basketball tournament. Each team must play one game with every team in the tournament. How many games altogether will be played in the tournament?

_____

Homework

Solve.

Show your work.

1. Sancho practices his trumpet every day from quarter to 5 to quarter past 5. How many minutes a day does he practice? How many hours?

   _____

2. Ella and her brother are going to a movie. It starts at quarter past 5 and lasts $2\frac{1}{4}$ hours. At what time will the movie end?

   _____

3. Jenn has soccer practice for $\frac{3}{4}$ of an hour on Tuesdays and Thursdays, and a game that lasts for about 1 hour on Saturdays. How many hours does she spend at soccer each week?

   _____

4. Before a storm, the outside temperature was 65°F. The storm caused the temperature to drop by 21°F. What was the outside temperature after the storm?

   _____

5. Write and solve your own word problem about time or temperature.

   _____

   _____

   _____

   _____

   _____

Remembering

Solve on a separate sheet of paper.

1. 6 × 80
2. 3 × 139
3. 37 × 18
4. 7 × 900

5. 5 × 228
6. 25 × 25
7. 3 × 4,000
8. 31 × 48

9. 46 × 85
10. 7 × 467
11. 45 × 14
12. 45 × 50

Find the surface area of each prism.

13.

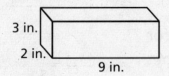

3 in.
2 in.
9 in.

_____

14.

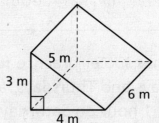

5 m
3 m
6 m
4 m

_____

Solve.

15. In Lian's collection of 42 stamps, $\frac{2}{3}$ of the stamps are from foreign countries. In Mark's collection of 42 stamps, $\frac{3}{7}$ of the stamps are from foreign countries. Who has collected the greater number of foreign stamps?

_____

16. Laura is $\frac{1}{7}$ as old as her grandfather. If her grandfather is 63 years old, how much older is her grandfather than Laura?

_____

Convert.

17. 4 in. = _____ ft
18. 6 yd = _____ ft

19. 8 oz = _____ lb
20. 2,500 lb = _____ t

21. 3 c = _____ fl oz
22. 6 qt = _____ gal

Homework

Write the missing percent or the missing numerator or denominator.

1. $65\% = \dfrac{65}{} = \dfrac{}{20}$

2. $80\% = \dfrac{}{100} = \dfrac{4}{}$

3. _____ $\% = \dfrac{30}{100} = \dfrac{}{10}$

4. _____ $\% = \dfrac{35}{100} = \dfrac{7}{}$

5. $\dfrac{2}{5} = \dfrac{}{100} =$ _____ %

6. $\dfrac{11}{20} = \dfrac{}{100} =$ _____ %

Write the equivalent decimal or percent.

7. $0.13 =$ _____ %

8. $0.05 =$ _____ %

9. $0.6 =$ _____ %

10. _____ $= 29\%$

11. _____ $= 6\%$

12. _____ $= 80\%$

Complete each row in the table by writing the missing numerators or percents.

	Fraction	Percent	Decimal
13.	$\dfrac{44}{100} = \dfrac{}{25}$	44%	_____
14.	$\dfrac{}{100}$	39%	_____
15.	$\dfrac{1}{4} = \dfrac{}{100}$	25%	_____

Solve.

16. Tara read 0.45 of her book. Marco read $\dfrac{3}{5}$ of his book. Calvin read 55% of his book. Each book has the same number of pages. Who has read the least number of pages? Explain how you found your answer.

_____

_____

Explain how to change a whole number, a decimal number in tenths, and a decimal number in hundredths, to a percent. Include an example of each change in your explanation.

_____

_____

_____

_____

_____

_____

_____

_____

_____

_____

_____

_____

_____

Homework

Use the unit rate to complete each table.

1.

Unit Rate: $4 per pound							
Pounds of Apples	1	2	3	4	5	6	7
Cost							

2.

Unit Rate: 65 miles per hour (mph)							
Time (in hours)	1	2	3	6	7	9	11
Distance (in miles)							

Use the table in exercise 1 to help solve each problem.

3. Shakira spent $36 on apples for her bakery. How many pounds of apples did she buy?

_____

4. Kyle has $55 to spend on 13 pounds of apples. Is this enough money to buy the apples? Explain.

_____

Use the table in exercise 2 to help solve each problem.

5. Antonio drove 260 miles at the given unit rate. For how many hours did he drive? _____

6. If George drives at a unit rate of 70 miles per hour, will he increase or decrease his average distance driven per hour? Give an example to support your answer.

_____

Solve.

7. The unit cost of one pencil is 17¢. What is the cost of twenty-three pencils? _____

8. A market sells 4 pounds of oranges for $12. What is the unit rate per pound for oranges? _____

9. A store sells a 7-ounce container of grape juice for $2.38 and a 15-ounce container for $4.80. Which container costs less per ounce? Explain.

_____

Homework

Write a situation that includes a rate that is not a unit rate. Explain why a unit rate would be easier to understand.

_____

_____

_____

_____

_____

_____

_____

_____

_____

_____

_____

_____

There are 24 students and 11 teachers on a bus. Use this information to write a ratio for each question.

1. What is the ratio of teachers to students? _____

2. What is the ratio of teachers to the total number of people on the bus? _____

Use the information in the exercises below to complete the ratio tables at the right. Then ask ratio questions of your classmates that can be answered using the tables.

3. Wayne is writing a book. The book will have 35 pages in each chapter. Complete Table 3 to show the number of chapters (c) for multiples of 35 pages (p).

4. The class is starting a new sewing project that uses 8 inches of red fabric for every 9 inches of blue fabric. In the first row of Table 4, write the ratio of inches of blue fabric (b) to inches of red fabric (r). Then complete Table 4.

5. Jacob uses 3 cups of raisins for every 2 cups of cherries. In the first row of Table 5, write the ratio of cups of raisins (r) to cups of cherries (c). Then complete Table 5.

Solve.

6. Carmen has 15 cups of water and 9 cups of milk. She needs to mix water and milk in the ratio of 4 cups of water to 3 cups of milk. What is the greatest amount of each ingredient that she can use?

_____

Table 3

(c)	(p)
1	35
3	
7	
	525
5	
	700

Table 4

(b)	(r)
45	
	24
	80
135	
99	

Table 5

(r)	(c)
	10
	16
30	
	24
	22

Name _____ **Date** _____

Homework

Write a situation that includes a ratio that is not
in simplest form. Explain why the simplest form of
the ratio would be easier to understand.

_____

_____

_____

_____

_____

_____

_____

_____

_____

_____

_____

_____

Ratios